400+ FUN & UNBELIEVABLE CHEERLEADING FACTS FOR KIDS

Contents

Introduction — 3
Chapter 1: History of Cheerleading — 4
Chapter 2: Famous Cheerleaders Around the World — 8
Chapter 3: Cheerleading Uniforms and Accessories — 11
Chapter 4: Cheerleading Stunts and Techniques — 14
Chapter 5: Cheerleading Competitions and Championships — 18
Chapter 6: Cheerleading Teams in Different Sports — 23
Chapter 7: Cheerleading Mascots and Their Roles — 27
Chapter 8: Cheerleading Chants, Cheers, and Routines — 31
Chapter 9: Cheerleading in Movies and TV Shows — 35
Chapter 10: Guinness World Records in Cheerleading — 39
Chapter 11: Cheerleading and Community Service — 43
Chapter 13: Cheerleading and School Spirit — 49
Chapter 14: Cheerleading Safety and Regulations — 52
Chapter 15: Cheerleading Brands and Equipment — 56
Chapter 16: Cheerleading in Different Countries and Cultures — 59
Chapter 17: Male Cheerleaders and Their Contributions — 64
Chapter 18: Cheerleading and Sportsmanship — 68
Chapter 19: Cheerleading and Fitness — 72
Chapter 20: Cheerleading Terminology and Slang — 75
Chapter 21: Cheerleading and Philanthropy — 78
Chapter 22: Cheerleading Superstitions and Traditions — 82
Chapter 23: Cheerleading Bloopers and Funny Moments — 86
Conclusion — 90

Introduction

Hey there, cheerleading fans! Get ready to dive into the exciting world of cheerleading with our fantastic collection of short stories that will make you laugh, cheer, and feel inspired! From the hilarious bloopers and funny moments that happen during practices and performances to the amazing ways cheerleaders help their communities through philanthropy and volunteering, we've got it all. You'll learn about the incredible stunts and routines that cheerleaders perform, the important role that fitness plays in their lives, and even some of the cool terminology and slang they use. But that's not all – we'll also introduce you to some of the most famous cheerleaders from around the world who have made a name for themselves both on and off the mat. You'll read about their incredible journeys and the challenges they've overcome to become the best of the best. And if you're dreaming of becoming a cheerleader yourself, we've got you covered with stories about the scholarships and opportunities available to help you reach your goals. So what are you waiting for? Get ready to jump, tumble, and cheer your way through these amazing stories that will leave you feeling energized, inspired, and ready to take on the world!

Chapter 1: History of Cheerleading

1. Did you know that cheerleading began as an all-male activity in the late 1800s? It wasn't until the 1920s that women started joining cheerleading squads.

2. The first recorded cheer was performed at Princeton University in 1884. It went like this: "Rah, Rah, Rah! Tiger, Tiger, Tiger! Sis, Sis, Sis! Boom, Boom, Boom! Aaaaah! Princeton, Princeton, Princeton!"

3. In the early days of cheerleading, the main purpose was to lead the crowd in cheers and chants to support their sports teams. Cheerleaders used megaphones, flags, and pom-poms to get the crowd excited.

4. The first cheerleading uniform was a turtle-neck sweater and a knee-length skirt, usually in the school colors. As cheerleading evolved, so did the uniforms, becoming more athletic and allowing for greater movement.

5. Lawrence Herkimer, known as the "grandfather of modern cheerleading," invented the pom-pom and established the first cheerleading camp in 1948. His innovations helped shape cheerleading into the sport we know today.

6. In the 1960s and 1970s, cheerleading began to incorporate more gymnastic elements, such as tumbling and stunts. This shift marked the beginning of cheerleading as a competitive sport.

7. The first televised national cheerleading competition took place in 1978 and was hosted by the International Cheerleading Foundation, now known as the World Cheerleading Association.

8. The 1980s saw a significant increase in the popularity of cheerleading. Many high schools and colleges across the United States formed their own cheerleading teams, and competitions became more frequent.

9. In 1997, ESPN first broadcast the National High School Cheerleading Championships, exposing cheerleading to a wider audience and helping to establish it as a legitimate sport.

10. Cheerleading has come a long way since its early days. Today, it is recognized as a competitive sport that requires athleticism, teamwork, and dedication.

11. The first African American cheerleader to cheer at the collegiate level was Brenda Edmonson Dublin. She joined the University of Mississippi cheerleading squad in 1968, breaking barriers during a time of racial segregation.

12. In 2004, the International Olympic Committee officially recognized cheerleading as a sport, paving the way for its potential inclusion in future Olympic Games.

13. The largest cheerleading uniform consists of a top and skirt measuring 9 meters tall and 15 meters wide. It was created by Fanshawe College students in London, Ontario, Canada, in 2011.

14. The longest cheerleading dance marathon lasted 30 hours and was achieved by the Bearden High School Varsity Cheerleaders in Knoxville, Tennessee, in 2011. The squad took turns performing their routine to raise money for charity.

15. In 2018, Kim Archie and Sarah Cronk co-founded the first cheerleading team for children with special needs. The Sparkle Effect has since grown to include over 200 teams across the United States.

16. The most consecutive back handsprings performed by a cheerleader is 44, a record set by Miranda Ferguson in 2017. Back handsprings are a common tumbling skill in cheerleading routines.

17. In 2020, the Netflix docuseries "Cheer" premiered, offering a behind-the-scenes look at the competitive world of collegiate cheerleading and bringing even more attention to the sport.

18. The first known use of the term "cheerleader" appeared in the November 2, 1897, edition of The Daily Princetonian, the student newspaper of Princeton University.

19. George W. Bush, the 43rd President of the United States, was a cheerleader during his high school years at Phillips Academy in Andover, Massachusetts.

20. The Dallas Cowboys Cheerleaders, one of the most famous cheerleading squads in the world, was founded in 1960. They have performed at numerous events and have been featured in several movies and TV shows.

Chapter 2: Famous Cheerleaders Around the World

1. Meryl Davis, an American ice dancer, was a cheerleader in middle and high school before winning an Olympic gold medal in 2014.

2. Actress Halle Berry was a cheerleader in high school and even competed in national championships before becoming a famous movie star.

3. Samuel L. Jackson, known for his roles in many movies, was a cheerleader at Morehouse College during his college years.

4. Ruth Bader Ginsburg, the late Supreme Court Justice, was a cheerleader in high school before becoming a powerful voice for women's rights.

5. Comedian and actor Steve Martin was a cheerleader at Garden Grove High School in California before making it big in Hollywood.

6. Madonna, the Queen of Pop, was a cheerleader in high school before becoming a global superstar and cultural icon.

7. Michael Douglas, an Oscar-winning actor, was a cheerleader at Choate Preparatory School in Connecticut during his high school years.

8. Ciara, a popular singer and dancer, was a cheerleader during her teenage years before launching her successful music career.

9. Sela Ward, an Emmy Award-winning actress, was a cheerleader at the University of Alabama before making it big on television.

10. Blake Lively, known for her role in "Gossip Girl," was a cheerleader in high school before becoming a famous actress.

11. Jayma Mays, an actress famous for her role in "Glee," was a cheerleader at Grundy High School in Virginia before pursuing acting.

12. Aaron Spelling, a well-known television producer, was a cheerleader at Southern Methodist University before creating hit TV shows.

13. Reba McEntire, a country music legend, was a cheerleader in high school in Oklahoma before becoming a successful singer.

14. Paula Abdul, a singer and former "American Idol" judge, was a cheerleader for the Los Angeles Lakers before her music career took off.

15. Fergie, a singer and member of the Black Eyed Peas, was a cheerleader in high school before achieving worldwide fame.

16. Megan Fox, an actress known for her role in "Transformers," was a cheerleader in high school before making it big in Hollywood.

17. Sandra Bullock, an Academy Award-winning actress, was a cheerleader in high school in Virginia before becoming a successful actress.

18. Jamie Foxx, an actor, comedian, and singer, was a cheerleader at Terrell High School in Texas before his entertainment career took off.

19. Alicia Silverstone, famous for her role in "Clueless," was a cheerleader in high school before becoming a well-known actress.

20. Olivia Munn, an actress and former television host, was a cheerleader at the University of Oklahoma before finding success in Hollywood.

Chapter 3: Cheerleading Uniforms and Accessories

1. Cheerleading uniforms often feature the school's colors and mascot to show team spirit and unity among the squad.

2. Skirts are a common part of cheerleading uniforms, allowing for easy movement and flexibility during routines and stunts.

3. Some cheerleading uniforms include shorts instead of skirts, providing a more athletic and comfortable look for the squad.

4. Sleeveless tops are popular in cheerleading uniforms to allow for a full range of motion during performances.

5. Many cheerleading uniforms have a unique design on the front, such as the school's initials or logo, to showcase pride.

6. Cheerleaders usually wear special shoes with good support and flexibility to help them perform jumps and stunts safely.

7. Pom-poms are a classic cheerleading accessory used to add visual interest and excitement to cheers and dance routines.

8. Some cheerleaders wear bows in their hair to match their uniforms and add an extra touch of spirit to their look.

9. Cheerleading socks often have unique designs or feature the school's colors to complete the uniform and show unity.

10. Uniforms are made from stretchy, durable materials to withstand the demands of cheerleading and maintain their shape.

11. Some schools have special uniforms for competitions that are more sparkly and eye-catching to stand out from other teams.

12. Megaphones are sometimes used by cheerleaders to amplify their voices and lead the crowd in cheers and chants.

13. Cheerleading uniforms have evolved over time, with some teams now wearing crop tops and leggings for a modern look.

14. Uniforms are often personalized with each cheerleader's name or initials to add a special touch and sense of belonging.

15. Some cheerleaders wear body glitter or face stickers to add extra sparkle and excitement to their performance look.

16. Cheerleading jackets are popular for keeping warm before and after performances, and they often feature the school's logo.

17. Cheerleaders might wear temporary tattoos of their school's logo or mascot for special events or competitions.

18. Some teams have separate uniforms for home and away games, with slight variations in design or color.

19. Cheerleading uniforms are designed to be eye-catching and help the squad stand out in a crowd during games and events.

20. Many cheerleaders keep their uniforms as special mementos long after they finish school, remembering the memories and friendships made.

Chapter 4: Cheerleading Stunts and Techniques

1. The toe touch is a classic cheerleading jump where the cheerleader leaps into the air, extends their legs, and touches their toes with straight arms. This jump requires flexibility, strength, and practice to perfect.

2. The herkie is a jump named after Lawrence Herkimer, the founder of modern cheerleading. In this jump, one leg is bent and the other is straight, forming an "L" shape in the air. Cheerleaders often perform this jump in unison during routines.

3. The pike jump involves jumping straight up with legs together and reaching for the toes, keeping the legs as straight as possible. This jump showcases a cheerleader's flexibility and control.

4. The hurdler jump resembles a hurdler in action, with one leg extended forward and the other bent back. This jump requires balance and coordination to execute properly.

5. Thigh stands are a partner stunt where a cheerleader stands on another cheerleader's thighs. This stunt requires balance, trust, and communication between teammates to ensure safety and stability.

6. Shoulder sits involve a cheerleader sitting on another's shoulders, often performed during pyramids or as a transition move. The base must have strong legs and a stable stance to support the top cheerleader's weight.

7. The liberty stunt is when a flyer stands on one leg while holding their other foot at chest level. The base supports the flyer's foot with a fully extended arm, showcasing the flyer's balance and the base's strength.

8. A cupie is similar to a liberty, but the flyer's foot is held at shoulder level instead of chest level. This stunt requires more flexibility from the flyer and greater stability from the base.

9. The heel stretch is a flexibility stunt where the cheerleader grabs their heel and pulls their leg up behind their head. This stunt demonstrates the cheerleader's flexibility and control.

10. The scorpion stunt involves the cheerleader grabbing their foot and pulling it behind their head, creating a "scorpion" shape. This advanced stunt requires significant flexibility and strength.

11. A basket toss is a dynamic stunt where a group of bases toss a flyer high into the air and then catch them. Timing, coordination, and trust are essential for the success and safety of this stunt.

12. The cradle catch is a dismount from a stunt where the flyer is caught in a cradle position by the bases. Clear communication and proper technique ensure a smooth and safe landing.

13. The extension is a stunt where a base lifts a flyer above their head with arms fully extended. This stunt showcases the base's strength and the flyer's balance and body control.

14. A pyramid is a formation involving multiple stunts and cheerleaders, creating a visually impressive display of teamwork. Pyramids require careful planning, coordination, and trust among all team members.

15. The back walkover is a gymnastics move incorporated into cheerleading, where the cheerleader arches back and steps over their hands. This move requires flexibility, balance, and core strength.

16. The back handspring is a dynamic tumbling skill where the cheerleader jumps backwards onto their hands and then springs back onto their feet. This skill takes practice and proper technique to master.

17. A round-off is a fundamental tumbling skill that involves a half-turn and a push off the ground with both feet, landing facing the opposite direction. This skill is often used as a setup for other tumbling passes.

18. The back tuck is a backflip with knees tucked into the chest, requiring power, technique, and spatial awareness to execute properly. Cheerleaders must practice this skill with proper safety measures and progression.

19. Stunting requires strong communication and trust between teammates to ensure safety and synchronization. Cheerleaders must work together and support one another both physically and emotionally.

20. Proper technique, practice, and safety measures are essential when learning and performing cheerleading stunts and skills. Coaches and experienced cheerleaders should always prioritize safety and provide guidance to help everyone improve and succeed.

Chapter 5: Cheerleading Competitions and Championships

1. The National High School Cheerleading Championship is the most prestigious competition for high school cheerleaders in the United States. Teams from all over the country compete in various categories to showcase their skills and teamwork.

2. The Universal Cheerleaders Association (UCA) hosts annual competitions for college cheerleading teams. These events feature impressive stunts, pyramids, and routines that highlight the athleticism and dedication of college cheerleaders.

3. The Cheerleading Worlds is an international competition where the best cheerleading teams from around the globe come together to compete for the title of world champion. This event showcases the highest level of skill and creativity in the sport.

4. The National Cheerleaders Association (NCA) All-Star National Championship is a competition for all-star cheerleading teams not affiliated with schools. These teams often feature advanced stunts and tumbling skills.

5. The USASF Cheerleading Worlds is another international competition that focuses on all-star cheerleading teams. This event attracts teams from various countries who compete in different age divisions and skill levels.

6. The European Cheerleading Championships is a competition held annually for European cheerleading teams. This event helps promote the growth and development of cheerleading in Europe.

7. The Asian Cheerleading Championships is a competition that showcases the talent of cheerleaders from Asian countries. This event helps foster cultural exchange and sportsmanship among participants.

8. The ICU World Cheerleading Championships is an event organized by the International Cheer Union, the governing body for cheerleading worldwide. This competition features teams from over 70 countries competing in various categories.

9. The NAIA Competitive Cheer & Dance National Championship is a competition for cheerleading and dance teams from smaller colleges and universities in the United States. This event recognizes the talent and dedication of these teams.

10. The Youth Cheerleading Nationals is a competition for younger cheerleaders, typically aged 5-14. This event provides an opportunity for young athletes to experience the excitement of competition and showcase their skills.

11. The Cheerleading Summit is a prestigious competition for all-star cheerleading teams. This event features a unique format where teams compete in a semi-final round before advancing to the finals.

12. The Cheersport National Cheerleading & Dance Championship is one of the largest competitions in the United States, attracting thousands of athletes from across the country. This event features a wide range of divisions and categories.

13. The America's Cup Cheer & Dance Championship is an international competition that invites teams from North and South America to compete against each other. This event promotes unity and sportsmanship among the participating countries.

14. The Cheerleading Federation of India (CFI) National Championship is the biggest cheerleading competition in India. This event helps popularize the sport in the country and encourages more young people to get involved.

15. The PanAmerican Cheerleading Championships is a competition for teams from countries in North, Central, and South America. This event showcases the diverse styles and traditions of cheerleading across the Americas.

16. The Australian All Star Cheerleading Federation (AASCF) National Championships is the largest cheerleading competition in Australia. This event features teams from all over the country competing in various levels and categories.

17. The New Zealand Cheerleading Nationals is an annual competition that brings together the best cheerleading teams from across New Zealand. This event helps promote the growth and development of the sport in the country.

18. The Canadian National Cheerleading Championships is the most significant cheerleading competition in Canada. This event features teams from all provinces and territories competing in different divisions and categories.

19. The African Cheerleading Championships is a competition that aims to promote and develop cheerleading in Africa. This event brings together teams from various African countries to compete and learn from each other.

20. The South American Cheerleading Championships is a competition that showcases the talent and passion of cheerleaders from South American countries. This event helps foster a sense of community and sportsmanship among the participating teams.

Chapter 6: Cheerleading Teams in Different Sports

1. Football cheerleaders are a common sight at high school and college games. They help pump up the crowd and support their team with energetic cheers and stunts.

2. Basketball cheerleaders have to be quick on their feet, as the fast-paced nature of the game means they must adapt their routines to keep up with the action.

3. Volleyball cheerleaders often incorporate the sport's moves into their routines, like mimicking a spike or a serve to engage the crowd and show support for their team.

4. Soccer cheerleaders have to be prepared for all types of weather, as they cheer on their team through rain, wind, and shine.

5. Ice hockey cheerleaders brave the cold temperatures of the rink to support their team, often wearing gloves and warm outfits to stay comfortable during games.

6. Rugby cheerleaders are a growing presence at matches, bringing energy and enthusiasm to a sport known for its toughness and physicality.

7. Baseball and softball cheerleaders keep the crowd engaged during the slower moments of the game, like between innings or during pitching changes.

8. Lacrosse cheerleaders have to be mindful of the fast-moving ball and players as they perform their routines along the sidelines.

9. Swimming and diving cheerleaders have a unique challenge, as they must find ways to cheer on their team without being too close to the pool deck.

10. Track and field cheerleaders support their team during meets, cheering on runners, jumpers, and throwers as they compete in various events.

11. Tennis cheerleaders must be respectful of the sport's etiquette, cheering loudly during breaks in play but remaining quiet during points.

12. Gymnastics cheerleaders incorporate many of the sport's moves into their routines, like tumbling and acrobatics, to showcase their own skills while supporting their team.

13. Wrestling cheerleaders must adapt their routines to the limited space around the mat, while still finding ways to engage the crowd and support their team.

14. Water polo cheerleaders face the challenge of cheering for a sport played in a pool, often coming up with creative ways to show their support from the sidelines.

15. Fencing cheerleaders must be mindful of the unique scoring system and pace of the sport as they cheer on their team during bouts.

16. Field hockey cheerleaders must be aware of the fast-moving ball and players as they perform routines along the sidelines of the pitch.

17. Badminton cheerleaders support their team during matches, often incorporating the sport's quick movements and jumps into their cheers and routines.

18. Table tennis cheerleaders must find ways to cheer on their team in a relatively quiet and focused environment, while still showing their support and enthusiasm.

19. Squash cheerleaders have to adapt their routines to the confined space of the court, while still finding ways to engage the crowd and support their team.

20. Ultimate Frisbee cheerleaders bring energy and enthusiasm to a sport that values sportsmanship and fair play, supporting their team through exciting matches and tournaments.

Chapter 7: Cheerleading Mascots and Their Roles

1. The Wildcats' mascot, Whiskers, loves to dance and do cartwheels along with the cheerleaders during games. His lively presence helps keep the crowd excited and engaged.

2. The Eagles' mascot, Swoop, is known for his high-flying stunts and acrobatics. He often joins the cheerleaders in their pyramid formations, adding an extra element of excitement to their routines.

3. The Tigers' mascot, Stripes, is always ready to give a high-five or pose for a photo with young fans. His friendly demeanor makes him a beloved figure among the team's supporters.

4. The Bulldogs' mascot, Buster, is famous for his silly antics and comedic skits during breaks in the game. He often teams up with the cheerleaders to entertain the crowd and keep spirits high.

5. The Panthers' mascot, Prowler, is an impressive dancer who often leads the crowd in choreographed cheers and chants. His smooth moves and energetic presence make him a fan favorite.

6. The Sharks' mascot, Finn, is known for his larger-than-life personality and love of the spotlight. He often steals the show during the cheerleaders' halftime performances with his wacky dance moves and humor.

7. The Lions' mascot, Roary, is a master of crowd interaction. He spends much of the game roaming the stands, high-fiving fans and leading cheers with the help of the cheerleaders.

8. The Bears' mascot, Grizz, is a gentle giant who loves to give hugs and take photos with young fans. His warm presence and friendship with the cheerleaders make him a beloved figure in the community.

9. The Rams' mascot, Rampage, is known for his strength and power. He often helps the cheerleaders with their stunts and pyramid formations, showcasing his impressive athleticism.

10. The Bees' mascot, Buzz, is a lively character who loves to dance and interact with the crowd. He often joins the cheerleaders in their sideline routines, adding an extra buzz of excitement to the game.

11. The Wolves' mascot, Howler, is famous for his distinctive howl that echoes through the stadium. He works with the cheerleaders to lead the crowd in chants and cheers, creating a powerful atmosphere of team spirit.

12. The Falcons' mascot, Talon, is an acrobatic wonder who often performs stunning flips and tricks alongside the cheerleaders. His aerial skills make him a thrilling addition to any game.

13. The Dragons' mascot, Blaze, is known for his fiery personality and love of mischief. He often playfully teases the cheerleaders and engages in friendly competitions with them during breaks in the game.

14. The Stallions' mascot, Spirit, is a majestic figure who embodies the grace and power of his team. He often leads the cheerleaders onto the field before games, setting the tone for an exciting event.

15. The Owls' mascot, Hooty, is a wise and friendly presence at games. He often works with the cheerleaders to create clever skits and routines that entertain and educate the crowd.

16. The Cougars' mascot, Roar, is known for his powerful presence and impressive roar. He often joins the cheerleaders in their stunts and pyramid formations, adding an extra element of strength to their routines.

17. The Gators' mascot, Snappy, is a lively character who loves to dance and interact with fans. He often teams up with the cheerleaders to create fun and engaging routines that get the crowd excited.

18. The Cardinals' mascot, Red, is a beloved figure known for his bright plumage and friendly demeanor. He often joins the cheerleaders in their community outreach events, spreading joy and team spirit beyond the stadium.

19. The Huskies' mascot, Frost, is a cool and collected presence at games. He often works with the cheerleaders to create stunning visual displays and choreographed routines that showcase the team's unity and strength.

20. The Rockets' mascot, Booster, is a high-energy character who loves to pump up the crowd. He often joins the cheerleaders in their fast-paced routines and stunts, adding an extra burst of excitement to the game.

Chapter 8: Cheerleading Chants, Cheers, and Routines

1. "Go, fight, win!" is a classic cheer that encourages the team to give their best effort and come out victorious. Cheerleaders often use this chant to pump up the crowd and show their support.

2. The "Defense" cheer is used when the team is trying to stop the opposing team from scoring. Cheerleaders will chant, "D-E-F-E-N-S-E," to encourage their team to stay strong and focused.

3. The "Victory" cheer is performed after the team scores or makes a great play. Cheerleaders might chant, "V-I-C-T-O-R-Y, that's our team's battle cry!" to celebrate the moment.

4. The "Let's Go" cheer is a simple but effective way to get the crowd involved. Cheerleaders will chant, "Let's go, [team name], let's go!" and encourage fans to clap along.

5. The "We've Got Spirit" cheer is a fun way for cheerleaders to showcase their enthusiasm. They might chant, "We've got spirit, yes we do, we've got spirit, how 'bout you?" and point to the crowd to join in.

6. The "Touchdown" cheer is performed after the team scores a touchdown in football. Cheerleaders might do a special jump or stunt while chanting, "T-O-U-C-H-D-O-W-N, touchdown, [team name]!"

7. The "Basket Toss" cheer is often used during a timeout or break in the action. Cheerleaders will perform a high-flying stunt where one cheerleader is tossed in the air and caught by their teammates.

8. The "Pyramid" cheer is an impressive display of teamwork and strength. Cheerleaders will build a human pyramid, with each level showcasing a different stunt or pose.

9. The "Tumbling" cheer features cheerleaders performing a series of acrobatic moves, like flips, handsprings, and somersaults, in synchronization with each other.

10. The "Pom Pom" cheer is a visually exciting routine that involves cheerleaders using colorful pom poms to create patterns and shapes while dancing and chanting.

11. The "Kick Line" cheer is a classic move where cheerleaders line up and perform a series of high kicks in unison, often while chanting or singing.

12. The "Split Jump" cheer is a dynamic move that involves cheerleaders performing a split leap in the air, showcasing their flexibility and athleticism.

13. The "Round Off" cheer is a tumbling move that cheerleaders use to transition into other stunts or formations. It involves a half-turn and a push off the ground with both feet.

14. The "Liberty" cheer is a stunt where one cheerleader stands on another's extended hand, balancing on one foot while the other leg is lifted high in the air.

15. The "Herkie" cheer is a jump named after Lawrence Herkimer, the founder of modern cheerleading. It involves one leg extended straight out while the other is bent, forming a "K" shape.

16. The "Toe Touch" cheer is a jump where cheerleaders reach their toes with their hands while keeping their legs straight and extended in a "V" shape.

17. The "Scorpion" cheer is a stunt where one cheerleader holds their foot behind their head while being supported by another cheerleader.

18. The "Cupie" cheer is a stunt similar to the Liberty, but with the raised leg bent at the knee, forming a "cup" shape.

19. The "Heel Stretch" cheer is a stunt where one cheerleader holds their leg straight up in the air while being supported by another cheerleader.

20. The "Wolf Wall" cheer is a formation where cheerleaders create a solid wall of bodies, showcasing their strength and unity as a team.

Chapter 9: Cheerleading in Movies and TV Shows

1. In the movie "Bring It On," rival cheerleading squads compete against each other, showcasing impressive stunts and routines while learning important lessons about teamwork and sportsmanship.

2. The TV show "Glee" features a group of high school students who participate in a glee club and a cheerleading squad, balancing their passion for performing with the challenges of teenage life.

3. In the Disney Channel Original Movie "Jump In!", a young boxer discovers his love for double Dutch jump rope and joins a competitive team, learning valuable lessons about following his heart and working hard.

4. The TV series "Hellcats" follows a college student who joins the cheerleading team to maintain her scholarship, discovering a new passion and forming close friendships along the way.

5. In the movie "Fired Up!", two high school football players join the cheerleading squad to meet girls, but end up falling in love with the sport and learning the value of dedication and teamwork.

6. The Disney Channel Original Movie "Zombies" features a cheerleading squad that must learn to work together with zombie students, promoting themes of inclusion and acceptance.

7. In the TV show "One Tree Hill," several characters are involved in the high school cheerleading squad, showcasing the challenges and triumphs of balancing athletics with personal lives.

8. The movie "Sugar & Spice" follows a group of cheerleaders who turn to crime to support their friend, highlighting the strong bonds and loyalty within the squad.

9. In the TV series "Riverdale," the character Cheryl Blossom is the captain of the River Vixens cheerleading squad, using her position to assert her power and influence within the school.

10. The movie "Buffy the Vampire Slayer" features the title character as a cheerleader who discovers her destiny as a vampire slayer, balancing her supernatural duties with her high school life.

11. In the TV show "Heroes," the character Claire Bennet is a high school cheerleader who discovers she has regenerative healing abilities, using her powers to help others while keeping her secret.

12. The movie "The Replacements" includes a subplot about cheerleaders who go on strike, leading to a group of misfits stepping in to take their place and learning the value of teamwork.

13. In the TV series "Sabrina the Teenage Witch," Sabrina joins the cheerleading squad and uses her magical powers to help her team, learning important lessons about responsibility and fairness.

14. The movie "Grease" features the character Sandy Olsson transforming from a shy student into a confident member of the cheerleading squad, showcasing the positive impact of friendship and self-discovery.

15. In the TV show "Gossip Girl," the character Serena van der Woodsen returns to school and joins the cheerleading squad, navigating the complex social dynamics of her elite private school.

16. The Disney Channel Original Movie "Cheetah Girls: One World" includes a cheerleading subplot, showcasing the importance of self-expression and staying true to oneself.

17. In the TV series "The Secret Life of the American Teenager," the character Grace Bowman is a cheerleader who faces personal challenges and grows in her faith and relationships.

18. The movie "17 Again" features a scene where the main character, in his teenage body, joins the cheerleading squad to get closer to his daughter, highlighting the importance of family bonds.

19. In the TV show "Smallville," the character Lana Lang is a cheerleader who becomes close friends with Clark Kent, showcasing the value of friendship and support.

20. The movie "Crooked Arrows" follows a Native American lacrosse team and includes a subplot about the team's cheerleaders, promoting themes of cultural pride and unity.

Chapter 10: Guinness World Records in Cheerleading

1. In 2019, the most cheerleaders performing simultaneous back handsprings was achieved by 22 cheerleaders from the Ace All Stars in Ohio, USA.

2. The longest cheerleading dance marathon lasted 30 hours and was achieved by the Bearden High School Varsity Cheerleaders in Knoxville, Tennessee, USA, in 2011.

3. The largest cheerleading dance consisted of 1,278 participants and was achieved by the United Spirit Association in Long Beach, California, USA, in 2016.

4. The most cheerleaders performing simultaneous toe touch jumps was 297, achieved by the Ohio State University in Columbus, Ohio, USA, in 2015.

5. The largest cheerleading poster measured 56.06 square meters (603.5 square feet) and was created by the Houston Texans Cheerleaders in Houston, Texas, USA, in 2017.

6. The most consecutive cartwheels performed by a cheerleader was 44, achieved by Julianna Hane in Wichita, Kansas, USA, in 2017.

7. The highest throw and catch of a cheerleader was 5.87 meters (19 feet 3 inches), achieved by the Top Gun All Stars in Miami, Florida, USA, in 2017.

8. The largest gathering of cheerleaders was 44,894, achieved at the 2018 Pyeongchang Winter Olympics in Pyeongchang, South Korea.

9. The most consecutive handsprings performed by a cheerleader was 46, achieved by Miranda Ferguson in Austin, Texas, USA, in 2017.

10. The largest cheer dance involved 3,849 participants and was achieved at an event organized by the Japan Cheerleading Association in Tokyo, Japan, in 2015.

11. The most consecutive back flips performed by a cheerleader was 37, achieved by Angel Rice in Miami, Florida, USA, in 2017.

12. The highest basket toss was 6.71 meters (22 feet), achieved by the Cheer Athletics Wildcats in Plano, Texas, USA, in 2019.

13. The most double full twists performed in 30 seconds by a cheerleader was 10, achieved by Alexandria Trevino in San Antonio, Texas, USA, in 2017.

14. The longest time balancing in a scorpion position by a cheerleader was 16.17 seconds, achieved by Makayla Pirtle in Houston, Texas, USA, in 2018.

15. The most twists performed in a single jump by a cheerleader was 4, achieved by Deiondra Sanders in Baton Rouge, Louisiana, USA, in 2018.

16. The most consecutive split jumps performed by a cheerleader was 49, achieved by Erika Erickson in Cincinnati, Ohio, USA, in 2017.

17. The most heel stretch rotations performed in 30 seconds by a cheerleader was 20, achieved by Jamie Andries in San Antonio, Texas, USA, in 2019.

18. The longest continuous cheer performed by a squad lasted 30 hours and 34 minutes, achieved by the Central High School Cheerleaders in Moulton, Alabama, USA, in 2014.

19. The most double nine stretch rotations performed in one minute by a cheerleader was 40, achieved by Cristian Nunez in Santiago, Chile, in 2018.

20. The fastest time to perform 10 toe touch jumps by a cheerleader was 4.37 seconds, achieved by Corbin Green in Cleveland, Tennessee, USA, in 2019.

Chapter 11: Cheerleading and Community Service

1. Sarah attended a summer cheerleading camp where she learned new stunts and made friends with cheerleaders from other schools.

2. The Ultimate Cheer Camp offered a variety of classes, from tumbling to stunting, helping Michael improve his skills and confidence.

3. Emily's team participated in a cheer clinic hosted by a local university, where they learned new routines and got feedback from college cheerleaders.

4. At the All-Star Cheer Camp, Jessica worked on her jumps and flexibility, setting personal goals and achieving them by the end of the week.

5. The Cheer Tech Camp focused on teaching cheerleaders how to use technology to create and share cheer routines, and Liam enjoyed learning new skills.

6. Megan's squad attended a team-building cheer camp, where they participated in trust exercises and bonding activities to strengthen their friendships.

7. The Cheer Spirit Camp had a theme of "Kindness Matters," encouraging Ava and her teammates to spread positivity and support one another.

8. At the Elite Cheer Camp, Ethan worked with experienced coaches to perfect his tumbling technique and learn advanced stunts.

9. The Cheer Leader Camp focused on developing leadership skills, and Olivia learned how to be a better role model for her squad.

10. Mason attended a cheer clinic hosted by a famous cheerleading company, where he got to meet and learn from his cheerleading idols.

11. The Cheer Fun Camp had a variety of activities, from crafts to games, and Sophia enjoyed bonding with her teammates in a relaxed setting.

12. At the Cheer Fitness Camp, Noah learned about the importance of proper nutrition and exercise for cheerleaders, helping him maintain a healthy lifestyle.

13. The Cheer Magic Camp had a Harry Potter theme, and Ella enjoyed learning new routines inspired by the wizarding world.

14. At the Cheer Stars Clinic, Aiden worked on his performance skills, learning how to engage the crowd and showcase his personality on stage.

15. The Cheer Heroes Camp focused on community service, and Zoe's squad volunteered at a local animal shelter as part of their camp experience.

16. Lucas attended a cheer camp that specialized in partner stunting, where he learned new techniques and built trust with his stunt group.

17. The Cheer Adventure Camp included outdoor activities like hiking and swimming, and Lily enjoyed exploring nature with her teammates.

18. At the Cheer Legends Clinic, Nora had the opportunity to learn from former Olympic cheerleaders and hear their inspiring stories.

19. The Cheer Unity Camp brought together cheerleaders from different backgrounds, and Max learned the importance of diversity and inclusion within the cheer community.

20. At the Cheer Dreams Camp, Quinn set personal goals for the week and worked hard to achieve them, feeling proud of her progress and newfound confidence.

Chapter 12: Cheerleading and Personal Growth

1. Emma worked hard on her cheerleading skills and maintained good grades, earning a full scholarship to her dream college.

2. The National Cheerleaders Association offered a scholarship program for outstanding cheerleaders, and Liam applied to showcase his talents.

3. Sophia's dedication to cheerleading and community service helped her win a scholarship from a local non-profit organization.

4. The University of Champions offered cheerleading scholarships to incoming students, and Ava earned one through her impressive audition.

5. Noah's high school coach nominated him for a cheerleading scholarship, recognizing his leadership and sportsmanship.

6. The Cheer Dreams Foundation provided scholarships for cheerleaders from low-income families, and Isabella was grateful for the opportunity.

7. Ethan's state cheerleading association offered scholarships for graduating seniors, and he applied to help fund his college education.

8. Megan's exceptional tumbling skills caught the attention of a college recruiter, who offered her a cheerleading scholarship.

9. The Cheer Scholars program recognized students who excelled in both cheerleading and academics, and Oliver was honored to be selected.

10. Zoe's parents encouraged her to apply for cheerleading scholarships to help offset the cost of college tuition.

11. The Cheer Stars Scholarship was awarded to cheerleaders who demonstrated outstanding leadership, and Lily was a proud recipient.

12. Mason's dedication to improving his stunting techniques helped him earn a partial scholarship to a prestigious cheerleading program.

13. The Cheer Legacy Scholarship honored cheerleaders whose parents or siblings also cheered in college, and Ella was excited to continue the family tradition.

14. Aiden's coach helped him create a portfolio showcasing his cheerleading achievements, which he submitted with his scholarship applications.

15. The Cheer Equity Scholarship aimed to increase diversity in cheerleading, and Nora was grateful for the opportunity to pursue her passion.

16. Lucas's school offered a scholarship for cheerleaders who maintained a high GPA, and he worked hard to meet the requirements.

17. The Cheer Futures Scholarship provided funding for cheerleaders to attend camps and clinics, and Quinn used it to improve her skills.

18. Sarah's local business community offered scholarships for student-athletes, including cheerleaders, and she applied to gain their support.

19. The Cheer Ambassadors Scholarship recognized cheerleaders who promoted the sport in their communities, and Michael was honored for his efforts.

20. Emily's hard work and dedication to cheerleading throughout high school paid off when she received a full scholarship to her top college choice.

Chapter 13: Cheerleading and School Spirit

1. At Oakwood Elementary, the cheerleaders led a pep rally to get everyone excited for the big game, teaching the students fun chants and cheers.

2. The Hillside Middle School cheerleaders created posters and decorations to fill the halls with school spirit before the academic challenge.

3. Riverdale High's cheerleaders organized a spirit week, assigning each day a different theme like "Crazy Hat Day" and "School Colors Day."

4. The cheerleaders at Sunnyside Elementary performed a special routine at the school talent show, showcasing their skills and love for their school.

5. Lakeview Middle School's cheerleaders volunteered to face paint students before the big game, using the school colors and mascot.

6. The Mountainview High cheerleaders led a charity fundraiser, challenging each grade to collect the most pennies for a local children's hospital.

7. Valleydale Elementary's cheerleaders created a spirit dance for students to perform during recess, promoting unity and fun.

8. The cheerleaders at Brookside Middle School organized a "Teacher Appreciation Day," decorating the teachers' lounge and providing breakfast.

9. Ridgecrest High's cheerleaders held a pep rally to honor students who had perfect attendance, celebrating their dedication to education.

10. The cheerleaders at Willowbrook Elementary led a "Kindness Campaign," encouraging students to perform random acts of kindness throughout the week.

11. Pinecrest Middle School's cheerleaders created a spirit tunnel for the soccer team to run through before their championship game.

12. The cheerleaders at Cedarwood High organized a "Multicultural Day," celebrating the diverse backgrounds of students and staff.

13. Maplewood Elementary's cheerleaders led a "Reading Rally," motivating students to read more books and earn prizes.

14. The cheerleaders at Oakridge Middle School created a spirit video, highlighting school events and showcasing student talents.

15. Elmwood High's cheerleaders organized a "Gratitude Week," encouraging students to write thank-you notes to teachers, staff, and peers.

16. The cheerleaders at Birchwood Elementary led a "Jump Rope for Heart" event, promoting physical fitness and raising money for heart health.

17. Cherrywood Middle School's cheerleaders created a spirit calendar, assigning each month a different theme and planning related activities.

18. The cheerleaders at Maplecrest High organized a "Staff vs. Students" volleyball game, promoting friendly competition and school unity.

19. Willowdale Elementary's cheerleaders led a "Spirit Parade," with each class creating a float to showcase their grade's unique personality.

20. The cheerleaders at Cedarcrest Middle School created a spirit mascot, taking turns wearing the costume and spreading cheer throughout the school.

Chapter 14: Cheerleading Safety and Regulations

1. Coach Emma always emphasized the importance of proper stretching before practice to help prevent injuries like strained muscles or sprains.

2. The Westfield High School cheerleading squad learned about using correct techniques when performing stunts to minimize the risk of accidents.

3. The cheerleaders at Oakdale Middle School participated in a safety workshop to learn about proper spotting methods and emergency protocols.

4. During practice, the Pinewood Elementary School cheerleaders always used mats to provide a softer landing surface and reduce the risk of injuries.

5. Coach Liam implemented a strict policy requiring all cheerleaders to have spotters present when attempting new or advanced stunts.

6. The Riverbend High School cheerleading team practiced their routines repeatedly until they could execute them safely and with confidence.

7. The Sunnyside Middle School cheerleaders learned about the crucial role of clear communication during stunts to ensure everyone was working together effectively.

8. Before every game, the Maplewood Elementary School cheerleaders performed a thorough warm-up routine to help prevent injuries and enhance their performance.

9. Coach Ava made sure the cheerleaders took regular water breaks and stayed hydrated throughout practice, particularly on hot and humid days.

10. The Cedar Creek High School cheerleading team implemented a buddy system, pairing each cheerleader with a partner to monitor each other's safety.

11. The Willowbrook Middle School cheerleaders received instruction on proper tumbling and landing techniques to minimize the risk of injury during floor routines.

12. When learning new skills, the Greenfield Elementary School cheerleaders always followed a step-by-step progression, mastering the basics before moving on to more advanced elements.

13. Coach Noah taught the cheerleaders specific conditioning exercises to help strengthen their bodies and prepare them for the physical demands of the sport.

14. The Lakeside High School cheerleading team conducted regular equipment inspections to ensure all materials were in good condition and safe to use.

15. The Oakwood Middle School cheerleaders learned about the importance of building trust and working collaboratively when performing group stunts and pyramids.

16. The Pineridge Elementary School cheerleading squad adhered to a strict dress code that ensured their uniforms allowed for a full range of motion and safe movement.

17. Coach Sophia educated the cheerleaders about proper nutrition and healthy eating habits to support their physical performance and overall well-being.

18. The Cedarwood High School cheerleading team regularly practiced emergency response drills to prepare them for handling potential accidents or injuries.

19. The Maplehurst Middle School cheerleaders learned to listen to their bodies and avoid overexerting themselves to prevent burnout and reduce the risk of injury.

20. The Elmwood Elementary School cheerleading squad celebrated safety milestones, acknowledging the team's commitment to following best practices and maintaining a safe environment.

Chapter 15: Cheerleading Brands and Equipment

1. Sarah loved her new Varsity cheerleading uniform, which was made with stretchy, breathable fabric that allowed her to move easily during routines.

2. Michael's Nfinity cheer shoes had extra support and cushioning, helping him land jumps and tumbling passes safely.

3. Emily was excited to try out her new Chassé practice wear, which included a comfortable tank top and shorts in her school colors.

4. The Stunt Stand practice mat helped Jessica's squad practice their stunts and pyramids safely, even when they weren't on the main gym floor.

5. Liam's team used Pom Poms from Omni Cheer to add visual interest to their routines and engage the crowd.

6. Ava's coach recommended using a Toss Back for practicing basket tosses, allowing the team to work on their technique safely.

7. The Tumbl Trak inflatable tumbling mat gave Noah a safe, cushioned surface to practice his tumbling skills at home.

8. Olivia's squad used the Jumpsoles plyometric training system to improve their vertical jumps and increase their explosive power.

9. The Athletic Specialties megaphone helped Ethan project his voice and lead cheers during games, keeping the crowd engaged.

10. Sophia's team used the Stunt Strap to practice new stunts safely, providing support for the flyer as they learned proper technique.

11. The Champion Fingerless Cheer Gloves helped Megan maintain a good grip on her pom poms and kept her hands warm during outdoor events.

12. Mason's squad used the Cheer Flik mat to practice their tumbling and stunting skills safely, with added cushioning and support.

13. The Chasse Cheer Backpack had plenty of room for Ella to store her uniform, shoes, and other essentials for competitions and practices.

14. Aiden's team used the Paraclete Cheer Stand to practice their stunts at various heights safely and confidently.

15. The Cheer Bow from Kandi Kouture added the perfect finishing touch to Zoe's uniform, showcasing her squad's colors and style.

16. Lucas's squad used the Blocking Dummy from Resilite to practice their partner stunts and improve their technique.

17. The Cheer Zone Folding Panel Mat allowed Lily's team to create a safe, portable practice space for their stunts and routines.

18. Nora's coach recommended using the Cheerleading Company Conditioning System to help the squad build strength and flexibility safely.

19. The Cheerleading Megaphone from Cheerleading.com helped Quinn lead cheers and communicate with her teammates during practices and games.

20. Max's team used the Stunt Prop from Myosource Kinetic Bands to practice their stunts and improve their flexibility safely and effectively.

Chapter 16: Cheerleading in Different Countries and Cultures

1. In Japan, cheerleading often incorporates elements of traditional dance, such as the use of fans and precise, synchronized movements. The cheerleaders' performances blend modern athleticism with cultural traditions, creating a unique style of cheerleading that reflects Japan's heritage.

2. Mexican cheerleading teams frequently use colorful uniforms that reflect the vibrant culture of the country. These uniforms often feature traditional Mexican motifs, adding a festive flair to the cheerleaders' performances and showcasing their national pride.

3. South African cheerleaders often incorporate African dance moves and rhythms into their routines, celebrating their cultural heritage. The energetic dance styles infuse their performances with a distinctly South African flavor.

4. In Australia, cheerleading has gained popularity, with many schools and clubs forming teams to support various sports. Australian cheerleaders bring their unique sense of humor and laid-back attitude to their performances.

5. Cheerleading in Russia often emphasizes acrobatics and gymnastics, with teams performing impressive stunts and tumbling routines. Russian cheerleaders are known for their exceptional athleticism and precision.

6. In Brazil, cheerleaders often perform at soccer matches, energizing the crowd with their passionate cheers and dances. The routines incorporate elements of samba, capoeira, and other popular Brazilian dance styles.

7. Chinese cheerleading teams frequently incorporate elements of martial arts, such as kung fu, into their routines. The graceful yet powerful movements blend with the precision and athleticism of cheerleading.

8. Cheerleading in Germany has grown in popularity, with many teams participating in European competitions. German cheerleaders often incorporate elements of gymnastics and dance into their routines.

9. In India, cheerleading is a growing sport, with teams drawing inspiration from Bollywood dance and music. The cheerleaders' routines often feature colorful costumes, lively music, and energetic dance moves.

10. Canadian cheerleading teams often brave cold temperatures to support their teams at hockey games and other winter sports events. Despite the chilly conditions, Canadian cheerleaders bring warmth and enthusiasm to their performances.

11. Cheerleading in France has been influenced by American-style cheerleading, but teams often add their own unique flair and style. French cheerleaders incorporate elements of ballet and other classical dance forms into their routines.

12. In Nigeria, cheerleading is becoming increasingly popular, with teams incorporating African dance and music into their routines. Nigerian cheerleaders often use traditional instruments to create lively rhythms.

13. South Korean cheerleaders are known for their precise, synchronized routines and often perform at international sporting events. Their performances showcase the country's dedication to discipline and teamwork.

14. Cheerleading teams in Argentina often perform at basketball and volleyball games, showcasing their high-energy routines. Argentinian cheerleaders incorporate elements of tango and other traditional dance styles into their performances.

15. In the United Kingdom, cheerleading has been growing in popularity, with many universities and clubs forming teams. British cheerleaders often bring a sense of humor and playfulness to their routines.

16. Jamaican cheerleaders often incorporate Caribbean dance styles, such as reggae and dancehall, into their lively performances. The cheerleaders' routines feature colorful costumes, infectious rhythms, and high-energy moves.

17. Cheerleading in Thailand has been influenced by American-style cheerleading, but teams often add traditional Thai dance elements. Thai cheerleaders use intricate hand gestures and graceful movements inspired by classical Thai dance.

18. In Spain, cheerleading teams can be found supporting a variety of sports, from soccer to basketball. Spanish cheerleaders often incorporate elements of flamenco and other traditional dance styles into their routines.

19. Kenyan cheerleaders often incorporate African dance moves and chants into their routines, reflecting their cultural pride. The cheerleaders' energetic performances often feature traditional Kenyan clothing and call-and-response chants.

20. Cheerleading teams in New Zealand have been growing in number, with many schools and clubs embracing the sport. New Zealand cheerleaders often incorporate elements of Maori culture into their routines, such as the haka war dance.

Chapter 17: Male Cheerleaders and Their Contributions

1. Jack joined the cheerleading squad and quickly became known for his impressive tumbling skills, inspiring other boys to try out. His dedication and talent helped break down gender stereotypes in the sport.

2. Tom's strong base skills made him an essential part of the squad's stunts, proving that cheerleading is for everyone. His contributions helped the team succeed and showed that gender doesn't define ability.

3. As the first male cheerleader at his school, David showed that gender stereotypes have no place in sports. He paved the way for future generations of boys to pursue their passions without fear of judgment.

4. Ryan's dedication to cheerleading and his positive attitude helped unite the squad and improve their performance. His leadership and enthusiasm inspired his teammates to work harder and support one another.

5. Michael's background in gymnastics made him a valuable asset to the cheerleading team, contributing to their success at

competitions. His unique skills and perspective helped the squad develop innovative routines.

6. Kevin's hard work and determination earned him the respect of his teammates and coaches, regardless of his gender. He proved that passion and commitment are the keys to success in any sport.

7. As a male flyer, Chris amazed the crowd with his aerial stunts and graceful movements, challenging traditional gender roles. His performances showed that cheerleading is a sport for everyone.

8. Andrew's leadership skills and enthusiasm made him a great co-captain, working alongside his female counterpart to lead the squad. Together, they fostered a supportive and inclusive environment for all cheerleaders.

9. Mark's creativity and unique perspective helped the squad develop innovative routines that wowed the judges at competitions. His contributions showcased the value of diversity in cheerleading.

10. By joining the cheerleading squad, Jason showed that it's essential to follow your passions, no matter what others might think. His courage and determination inspired others to pursue their dreams.

11. Tyler's strength and agility made him a reliable base for the squad's most challenging stunts, ensuring his teammates' safety. His dedication to his role helped the team perform at their best.

12. As a male cheerleader, Brian used his platform to advocate for inclusivity and acceptance within the sport. He encouraged others to embrace diversity and challenge stereotypes.

13. Noah's positive energy and encouragement helped his teammates overcome their fears and try new skills, fostering a supportive environment. His leadership and compassion made him a valued member of the squad.

14. Ethan's dedication to mastering new techniques inspired his fellow cheerleaders to push themselves and strive for excellence. His hard work and passion set a positive example for the team.

15. Liam's ability to connect with the crowd during performances helped the squad engage with the audience and spread school spirit. His charisma and enthusiasm were infectious, both on and off the mat.

16. As the only male cheerleader on his team, Alex showed that true talent and passion know no gender boundaries. He broke down barriers and inspired others to follow their dreams.

17. Dylan's natural ability to lead by example motivated his teammates to work harder and support one another, on and off the mat. His leadership and dedication helped create a strong, united squad.

18. Owen's willingness to learn and grow as a cheerleader earned him the admiration and respect of his coaches and peers. His openness to feedback and desire to improve made him a valuable team member.

19. By participating in cheerleading, Carter challenged societal norms and encouraged other boys to pursue their interests without fear of judgment. His bravery and determination helped change perceptions about the sport.

20. As a pioneering male cheerleader, Logan paved the way for future generations of boys to experience the joy and camaraderie of the sport. His legacy inspired others to break down barriers and pursue their passions.

Chapter 18: Cheerleading and Sportsmanship

1. Sarah was told that cheerleaders were just pretty faces, but she knew that cheerleading required hard work, dedication, and athletic skill. She worked tirelessly to perfect her routines and prove that cheerleaders are true athletes.

2. Michael faced teasing from his classmates when he joined the cheerleading squad, but he didn't let their words discourage him. He knew that cheerleading was a challenging sport that required strength, flexibility, and teamwork.

3. Emily heard people say that cheerleaders weren't smart, but she knew better. She maintained excellent grades while dedicating herself to cheerleading, proving that cheerleaders can excel both academically and athletically.

4. David's friends thought that cheerleading was only for girls, but he showed them that boys could be incredible cheerleaders too. He became a skilled base, supporting his teammates and showcasing his athleticism.

5. Lily was told that cheerleaders were shallow and only cared about popularity, but she knew that her squad was filled with kind, supportive friends who worked hard and cared about each other.

6. Ethan's older brother teased him for being a cheerleader, saying it wasn't a real sport. But Ethan invited his brother to watch a competition, and he was amazed by the skill and dedication of the cheerleaders.

7. Olivia heard people say that cheerleaders were weak, but she knew the truth. She had seen her teammates power through tough practices, lift each other up, and support their school with unwavering spirit.

8. Ryan's parents were initially skeptical about him joining the cheerleading team, thinking it wouldn't be challenging enough. However, after seeing the complex routines and the effort required, they became his biggest supporters.

9. Sophie encountered people who thought cheerleaders were only there to look pretty, but she knew that her squad's primary purpose was to lead the crowd, support their team, and spread school spirit.

10. Andrew's classmates thought that cheerleading was easy, but he invited them to try a practice. After attempting the stunts and routines, they gained a new respect for the hard work and dedication required.

11. Megan faced stereotypes that cheerleaders were mean and exclusive, but she made it her mission to create a welcoming and supportive environment for all her teammates, regardless of their background or experience level.

12. Jacob's friends teased him for being a male cheerleader, but he knew that gender had no bearing on his ability to be a great athlete and teammate. He continued to pursue his passion with pride.

13. Ava's aunt assumed that cheerleading was just a popularity contest, but Ava explained that her squad was focused on supporting each other, improving their skills, and representing their school with pride.

14. Nathan knew that some people thought cheerleading was frivolous, but he saw the important role it played in boosting school spirit, uniting the student body, and creating a positive atmosphere at events.

15. Grace heard people dismiss cheerleading as "not a real sport," but she knew the countless hours of practice, the physical demands, and the mental toughness required to excel in cheerleading competitions.

16. Owen's sister thought cheerleaders were just sideline entertainers, but he showed her how his squad's cheers and routines directly impacted the energy and motivation of the players on the field.

17. Lucy encountered the stereotype that cheerleaders were unintelligent, but she and her teammates were dedicated students who balanced their academic pursuits with their passion for cheerleading.

18. Max's grandparents were surprised to learn that cheerleading involved so much athleticism and teamwork, having previously thought of it as more of a social activity. Max enjoyed teaching them about the sport he loved.

19. Sophia's cousin assumed that all cheerleaders were the same, but Sophia's squad was a diverse group of individuals with unique personalities, backgrounds, and strengths that made them a strong, cohesive team.

20. Liam knew that some people thought cheerleading was all about looking good, but he and his teammates focused on developing their skills, supporting each other, and being positive role models in their community.

Chapter 19: Cheerleading and Fitness

1. Sarah's coach always emphasizes the importance of proper warm-ups and stretches before practice to prevent injuries and improve flexibility.

2. Liam's squad incorporates strength training exercises like push-ups and squats into their routines to build the muscle needed for stunts and tumbling.

3. Olivia's team starts each practice with a lap around the gym to get their heart rates up and build endurance for long performances.

4. Ethan's coach teaches the squad about the importance of staying hydrated during practices and competitions, encouraging them to drink plenty of water.

5. Ava's squad ends each practice with a cool-down session that includes yoga poses and deep breathing exercises to promote relaxation and recovery.

6. Noah's team includes cardio exercises like jumping jacks and high knees in their warm-ups to improve their stamina and energy levels.

7. Zoe's coach invites a nutritionist to speak to the squad about healthy eating habits that support their athletic performance and overall well-being.

8. Ryan's squad practices plyometric exercises like box jumps and bounding to develop the explosive power needed for jumps and tumbling passes.

9. Mia's team incorporates core-strengthening exercises like planks and Russian twists into their conditioning routines to improve balance and stability.

10. Adam's coach teaches the squad proper landing techniques to minimize the impact on their joints and reduce the risk of injuries.

11. Sophie's squad uses resistance bands to work on their leg strength and improve their flexibility for kicks and splits.

12. Emily's team includes a variety of dynamic stretches in their warm-ups to prepare their muscles for the demands of cheerleading.

13. Liam's coach encourages the squad to participate in cross-training activities like swimming and cycling to improve their overall fitness.

14. Isabella's squad practices yoga once a week to develop body awareness, balance, and mental focus.

15. Ryan's team uses foam rollers to massage their muscles and promote recovery after intense practices and competitions.

16. Olivia's coach teaches the squad about the importance of getting enough sleep and rest to support their athletic performance and physical health.

17. Ethan's squad incorporates agility drills like ladder exercises and cone drills into their practices to improve their speed and coordination.

18. Ava's team practices deep breathing exercises before competitions to calm their nerves and focus their energy.

19. Noah's coach encourages the squad to set personal fitness goals and track their progress throughout the season to stay motivated and accountable.

20. Zoe's squad celebrates their fitness achievements together, cheering each other on and supporting one another in their health and wellness journeys.

Chapter 20: Cheerleading Terminology and Slang

1. Sarah learned that a "cradle" is when a flyer is caught by her bases after a stunt, like being rocked in a baby's cradle.

2. Liam's coach taught him that "facials" refer to the cheerleaders' expressions during a routine, not a spa treatment for their skin.

3. Olivia giggled when she heard the term "peel off," imagining cheerleaders peeling like bananas, but learned it's when they leave the formation.

4. Ethan practiced his "touchdown" motion, not by scoring a football goal, but by raising his arms straight up for a cheer.

5. Ava learned that a "liberty" is not just a statue, but a stunt where a flyer stands on one leg while holding the other.

6. Noah's coach reminded him to "squeeze" during stunts, not like a teddy bear, but to engage his muscles for stability.

7. Zoe found it funny that "pop" can mean a sudden, sharp motion in cheerleading, not just a fizzy drink.

8. Ryan learned that "full downs" are not a sad feeling, but a type of push-up used for conditioning in cheerleading.

9. Mia practiced her "herkie," not a dance move from the 60s, but a jump named after Lawrence Herkimer, the father of modern cheerleading.

10. Adam's squad celebrated their "hit" routine, not by punching it, but by executing it perfectly from start to finish.

11. Sophie learned that "banana rolls" are not a dessert, but a type of tumbling drill used to practice body control.

12. Emily's coach taught her to "whip" her arms, not like cracking a whip, but by moving them sharply for momentum in jumps.

13. Liam chuckled when he heard "sushi roll," thinking of his favorite snack, but learned it's a tumbling move where cheerleaders roll sideways.

14. Isabella practiced her "wolf wall," not by howling at the moon, but by forming a line with her squad for a synchronized stunt.

15. Ryan's coach reminded him to "lock" his arms, not with a key, but by keeping them straight and strong during stunts.

16. Olivia learned that a "waterfall" in cheerleading is not a cascading stream, but a formation where cheerleaders connect to make a wavy line.

17. Ethan's squad celebrated their "butter" landing, not by spreading it on toast, but by sticking a landing smoothly and effortlessly.

18. Ava practiced her "kewpie," not a type of doll, but a stunt where a flyer stands on one leg with the other bent.

19. Noah's coach encouraged him to "punch" his motions, not by hitting them, but by making them sharp and precise.

20. Zoe learned that "hitting" the mat is not a form of aggression, but a way to describe the moment a cheerleader lands a tumbling pass.

Chapter 21: Cheerleading and Philanthropy

1. Sarah's cheerleading squad organized a bake sale to raise money for a local animal shelter, helping to provide food and medical care for the animals.

2. Liam's team participated in a charity walk to raise funds for a children's hospital, cheering on the participants and helping to create a festive atmosphere.

3. Olivia's squad volunteered at a local food bank, sorting donations and packing meals for families in need, learning the importance of giving back to their community.

4. Ethan's team held a car wash fundraiser to support a local homeless shelter, providing essential supplies and resources for those in need.

5. Ava's squad organized a toy drive during the holiday season, collecting new toys to donate to children from low-income families, spreading joy and cheer.

6. Noah's team participated in a charity cheer competition, with proceeds going to support a local youth center, providing a safe space for children to learn and grow.

7. Zoe's squad volunteered at a Special Olympics event, cheering on the athletes and helping to create a supportive and inclusive environment.

8. Ryan's team organized a school supply drive, collecting backpacks, notebooks, and other essentials for students in need, ensuring everyone had the tools to succeed.

9. Mia's squad held a bake sale to raise money for a local charity that provides meals to seniors, helping to combat hunger and isolation in their community.

10. Adam's team participated in a charity dance marathon, raising funds for a local children's advocacy center, supporting victims of abuse and neglect.

11. Sophie's squad volunteered at a local nursing home, performing routines and spending time with the residents, bringing smiles and companionship to the elderly.

12. Emily's team organized a clothing drive, collecting gently used coats and shoes to donate to a local family shelter, providing warmth and comfort to those in need.

13. Liam's squad held a charity car wash to raise money for a local environmental organization, supporting efforts to preserve and protect their community's natural resources.

14. Isabella's team participated in a charity obstacle course race, raising funds for a local youth sports program, promoting physical fitness and teamwork.

15. Ryan's squad volunteered at a local community garden, planting vegetables and herbs to be donated to a food pantry, promoting access to fresh, healthy food.

16. Olivia's team organized a pet supply drive, collecting food, toys, and bedding to donate to a local animal rescue organization, supporting the care of homeless pets.

17. Ethan's squad held a charity cheer clinic, teaching younger children basic skills and routines, with proceeds benefiting a local pediatric cancer foundation.

18. Ava's team participated in a charity talent show, showcasing their skills and raising money for a local arts program, supporting creative expression in their community.

19. Noah's squad volunteered at a local beach cleanup, removing litter and debris to protect marine life and preserve the natural beauty of their coastline.

20. Zoe's team organized a book drive, collecting new and gently used books to donate to a local children's literacy program, promoting the joy of reading and learning.

Chapter 22: Cheerleading Superstitions and Traditions

1. The Westfield Warriors always braided each other's hair before competitions, believing it brought them good luck and kept their team united.

2. Olivia's squad had a tradition of writing their goals on ribbons and tying them to their shoes before every performance, as a reminder to strive for excellence.

3. The Riverdale Rockets never washed their uniform socks during the competition season, convinced that the "lucky" socks helped them perform their best.

4. Liam always ate a peanut butter and banana sandwich before games, believing it gave him the energy and focus he needed to lead his squad.

5. The Sunnyside Sharks had a pre-performance ritual of forming a circle, holding hands, and reciting a positive affirmation together to boost their confidence.

6. Sophie never stepped on the performance mat with her left foot first, convinced that starting with her right foot brought her squad good luck.

7. The Maplewood Bears always passed a sparkly baton around the team before competitions, with each cheerleader making a wish for the team's success.

8. Ethan's squad had a tradition of hiding a small stuffed animal mascot in their coach's bag before every competition, believing it brought them good fortune.

9. The Cedarwood Cardinals always chanted "1, 2, 3, Cardinals!" before taking the stage, a tradition that pumped them up and showed their team pride.

10. Isabella never performed without wearing her lucky hair bow, which she believed helped her execute her stunts and tumbling passes flawlessly.

11. The Willowbrook Wildcats had a tradition of painting a paw print on their cheeks before every game, symbolizing their team unity and fierce spirit.

12. Ryan always double-knotted his shoelaces before performing, a superstition he believed kept him safe and prevented him from tripping during routines.

13. The Grassland Gators had a pre-game tradition of linking pinkies and making a wish together, a ritual they believed brought them luck and success.

14. Zoe never chewed gum during competitions, convinced that it would make her lose focus and cause her to make mistakes in her routines.

15. The Ridgeview Rams always lined up in height order before taking the stage, a tradition they believed created a sense of harmony and unity.

16. Adam's squad had a tradition of giving each other high-fives and saying "You've got this!" before each cheerleader's individual performance.

17. The Elmwood Eagles never said the word "fall" on competition day, believing that it would jinx their performances and cause them to make mistakes.

18. Ava always wore mismatched socks during competitions, a superstition she believed brought her good luck and helped her perform her best.

19. The Pinehill Panthers had a tradition of doing a silly dance together before every game, a ritual that helped them relax and bond as a team.

20. Noah's squad always ended their practices with a group hug, a tradition that symbolized their love and support for one another, both on and off the mat.

Chapter 23: Cheerleading Bloopers and Funny Moments

1. During a pep rally, Sophie's pom-pom flew out of her hand and landed on the principal's head, causing everyone to giggle.

2. Liam's squad tried a new pyramid formation, but when they dismounted, they all fell down like dominoes, laughing as they untangled themselves.

3. Olivia's team was performing a cheer when suddenly, a gust of wind blew their skirts up, revealing their colorful bloomers and making the crowd chuckle.

4. During a timeout, Ethan's squad started a wave, but when it came back around, they all did different moves, creating a hilarious display of uncoordinated enthusiasm.

5. Ava accidentally stepped on her own shoelace during a routine, causing her to stumble and do a silly dance to regain her balance, making her teammates smile.

6. Noah's team was practicing a new chant when one cheerleader sneezed mid-cheer, creating a domino effect of laughter and "bless you's" throughout the squad.

7. During a football game, Ryan's squad was so focused on their cheers that they didn't realize the game had ended, continuing to chant as the crowd giggled.

8. Zoe's team was performing a dance routine when one cheerleader's hair tie broke, causing her hair to fly wildly as she danced, creating a comical sight.

9. Adam's squad was practicing a stunt when their flyer sneezed, causing the bases to lose their grip and everyone to fall into a laughing heap.

10. Isabella's team was lined up for a serious photo when one cheerleader made a silly face, causing a chain reaction of laughter and goofy poses.

11. During a basketball game, Mia's squad was cheering so loudly that they didn't hear the buzzer, continuing to chant as the players ran off the court.

12. Sarah's team was learning a new cheer when one cheerleader accidentally said "funky" instead of "mighty," causing everyone to erupt in laughter.

13. Liam's squad was practicing a stunt when their flyer's shoe fell off, landing in the lap of a surprised spectator and causing everyone to chuckle.

14. Emily's team was performing a routine when one cheerleader's skirt got stuck on her pom-pom, creating a comical tug-of-war as she tried to free herself.

15. During a football game, Ethan's squad was so excited that they started cheering for the wrong team, realizing their mistake and quickly changing their chant.

16. Olivia's team was taking a water break when one cheerleader accidentally squirted water out of her nose, causing a chain reaction of laughter and spit-takes.

17. Ryan's squad was practicing a new dance move when one cheerleader tripped and fell into a split, making everyone gasp before erupting into applause.

18. Sophie's team was posing for a picture when a gust of wind blew their pom-poms into each other's faces, creating a hilarious and colorful photo.

19. During a pep rally, Noah's squad was performing a chant when one cheerleader's voice cracked, causing everyone to giggle and cheer even louder.

20. Ava's team was celebrating after a successful routine when they all went in for a group hug, accidentally knocking each other over and laughing as they fell.

Conclusion

Wow, what an incredible journey we've been on together through the world of cheerleading! From the side-splitting bloopers and funny moments that made us giggle to the heartwarming stories of cheerleaders giving back to their communities, we've seen it all. We've learned about the amazing athleticism and dedication it takes to perform those jaw-dropping stunts and routines, and how important it is for cheerleaders to take care of their bodies through proper fitness and nutrition. We've even picked up some cool new cheerleading terms and slang to impress our friends with! And let's not forget about the inspiring stories of famous cheerleaders who have paved the way for future generations, showing us that with hard work and determination, anything is possible. Whether you're a seasoned cheerleader or just starting out, these stories have shown us that cheerleading is so much more than just pom-poms and chants – it's a way to build friendships, develop valuable life skills, and make a positive impact on the world around us. So keep on cheering, keep on dreaming, and most importantly, keep on spreading that contagious spirit and enthusiasm that makes cheerleading so special. Who knows, maybe one day we'll be reading about your amazing cheerleading journey in a book just like this one!

Printed in Great Britain
by Amazon